Vyzoviti, Sophia
Folding Architecture: Spatial, Structural and
Organizational Diagrams

Gingko Press Inc.
5768 Paradise Drive, Suite J
Corte Madera, CA 94925, USA
T: +1 415 924 9615
F: +1 415 924 9608
books@gingkopress.com
www.gingkopress.com

ISBN 1-58423-204-8

Contents

Acknowledgements

Folding Architecture - Spatial, Structural and Organizational Diagrams, comprises a case study of folding as a generative process in architectural design. The case has been built on observation, documentation and analysis of the standard educational procedure of design studio D10: **Het Lab - Proeftuin voor Ontwerpen en Nieuwe Theorieën** that I have been instructing in the Faculty of Architecture, Delft University of Technology, with the status of guest teacher since 2000. Hans Cornelissen the D10 design studio course director has supported this research in the course of three academic years and contributed essentially to the design investigation and the publishing of this book. This publication has been granted the permission of Professor H. Beunderman, Dean of the Faculty of Architecture T.U.Delft. I would like to primarily thank all the students that seriously engaged with the studio research and especially the ones contributing to this publication: Trine Bang, Safia Benayard-Serif, Mattieu Bescaux, Paul-Eric Bonnans, Robert Bos, Marcus Buitenweg, Johan Cederlof, Fokke van Dijk, Moniek Haverkort, Andreas Lokitek, Fredrick Lyth, Daniel Norel, Tijs Pulles, Bas Rozenbeek, Thys Schreij, Joost van Boekhold, Christian Vedeler, Bas Vogelpoel, Cindy Wouters and Jerome Zwart.
The visual essay in *Folding as a Morphogenetic Process in Architectural Design - D10 Design Studio Case* Study primarily consists of photographic documentation of working models in all phases of the studio process. Hans Kruze, Hans Schouten, and myself, as well as several students are responsible for the photography. Joost van Boekhold and Gabriel Pena assisted me in the studio documentation of D10-2001. Joost Berkhout

provided precious graphic design consultancy. Pnina Avidar
sustained the further development of the research inviting me
to apply this explicit design method in the analysis and design
studio **In-Gewikkelde Ruimte** at Tilburg Academy for
Architecture and Urbanism in 2002. Marc Schoonderbeek, Olga
Vazquez-Ruano and Paul van der Voort contributed to additional
development during our collaboration in *The Hand Stays in the
Picture* workshop that took place in spring 2003 under the
MSc1-Studio **Border Conditions** at the same faculty.
Magnus Björkman, Ophelie Herranz, Paul Galindo and Natasha
Fricout have contributed to this publication with exercises
accomplished in this workshop. For editorial assistance, my
gratitude to Penelope Dean and Deborah Hauptmann.
All images included in the essay *Folding Architecture - Concise
Genealogy of the Practice* are courtesy of the architects
mentioned. A special mention to VMX architects and
video-artist Sander Meulmeester for their enthusiastic
submission of original imagery.

Prologue

The D10 design studio project is an example of an architectural design process with a circular nature. In contrast to a linear process, it allows one to encircle a problem and understand and confront it in all its relationships - in other words, it is a kind of exploration. It results among other things in an expansion from logical to associative coherence. The effect is investigative design and attitude formation. In this context, the fold is more important for the development of methods to arrive at a new architecture, than it is for the development of an individual architectural form.

Folding is relatively unknown to students, folding is a challenge with great individual possibilities. Opening a fold in a surface creates spaces, which in our minds are filled with volumes. Thus, the technique of folding makes it possible to re-appraise every step. Each step is laden with potential. Folding and the associated development of hand-eye co-ordination liberates the design thought-process from preconceptions and removes any existing architectonic images. The limitation that the technique of folding brings with it sharpens the mind and stimulates creativity. Folding also implicitly allows accidental and unknown end-results for a relatively long period of the design process. The enormous number of possibilities makes a choice necessary. Lines must be drawn in sometimes chaotic, yet remarkable, folding models. The scope, suitability and significance of these will be a subject for discussion. There are two observations to be made here: Folding is not concerned with creating a new style but rather with searching for links. Forms bring up the problem of human scale, as they can unconsciously display monumental characteristics. Working on

a larger scale makes this problem visible. This way of folding is more radical than origami because it includes no narrative element. The fold is a sort of affectionate space. More than just reason, meaning and function are involved here. The fold alters the traditional viewpoint. The incisions are no longer concerned with aesthetics or meaning but with a different type of order. Observing them can confuse the knowledge-hungry student.
Folding is more important for the development of techniques to derive new architecture than for the development of an individual
architectonic form. It is therefore, as Gilles Deleuze claims, an 'absolute internalisation.' The ambiguity, which characterises the
folding project, is unmistakable in the end result. These possibilities can be differently interpreted, accentuated and combined by each
individual; that is to say, a great difference between equally valid designs is noticeable, because everyone is different.
Folding produces a language of architecture. It is the strength of the architectonic
language that speaks out and determines the quality. The first folds must thus be viewed as sounds that only much later become words.
It is a new language, at least for the student, which must be learned.

Hans Cornelissen, D10 design studio course director

Folding as a Morphogenetic Process in Architectural Design

Folding as a generative process in architectural design is essentially experimental: agnostic, non-linear and bottom up. Our interest lies on the morphogenetic process, the sequence of transformations that affect the design object. Considering this an open and dynamic development where the design evolves with alternate periods of disequilibrium, we can appreciate the function of folding as a design generator by phase transitions, that is, critical thresholds where qualitative transformations occur. Cut off from the continuum of the studio process, four phase transitions are presented further illustrating the case with a visual essay: matter and functions, algorithms, spatial-structural-organizational diagrams and architectural prototypes.

Transition 1: Matter and Functions

Ivory Carton[1] is introduced as quintessential foldable material given the paper's weight and structural capacity. The task is to extensively explore transformations of a single paper surface into a volume, with one constraint only, maintaining the continuity of the material. The paper's transformative origins are simple actions, intuitive responses, delivered here as a list of verbs; fold, press, crease, pleat, score, cut, pull up, rotate, twist, revolve, wrap, pierce, hinge, knot, weave, compress, unfold. In the early folding performances, we can appreciate the paperfold[2] as a diagram in Deleuzian terms, an abstract machine knowing nothing of forms and substances; operating purely by matter and function[3]. Reading the paperfold as a diagram, that does not represent but rather constitutes a new type of reality introduces architectural research into a field of actualization.

Transition 2: Algorithms

The paperfold is a dynamic artefact, unstable and evolving. It bares the traces of the activity that brings it into being: scores, creases or incisions drawn in the surface of the paper. The paperfold unfolded, becomes a map of its origination process. Repetitive paper folding performances evolve initial intuitive responses into primary techniques: triangulation, stress forming, stratification of folds, folds within folds, or patterns like strips, spline curves, spirals, or meanders. Manipulation of paper surface in order to produce volume constitutes a curriculum of activity, a program. Paperfold generative transformations are structured in sequences. We consider the succession of transformations resulting to the paperfold artefact as a genetic algorithm of form. The task in this phase is to decipher the paperfold algorithm as a morphogenetic mechanism. Generative sequences, augmented techniques, unfolding, transformation mappings, instructive plans and inventories of transformation are submitted here as definitions of the paperfold algorithm. Understanding and developing the paperfold algorithm transgresses the singularity of the object spawning a series of similar but varying artefacts. This re-introduces the problem of documentation, requiring notation[4] as a set of instructions that include time as a variable. Thus the paperfold can be considered an event, defined by Leibniz[5] as an extension, where the object expands into an infinite series of variability containing neither a final term nor a limit.

Transition 3: Spatial, Structural and Organizational Diagrams

Space emerges in the paperfold during a dynamic volume generation process. The void bounded between the folds of the paper manifests a curvilinear form that cannot be exactly defined. Like its delimiting surfaces it manifests increased continuity despite its fragmentation. Mapping the paperfold as a spatial diagram requires an abstraction of spatial relations. Geometric characteristics are initially irrelevant. Topological properties are crucial to describe the space emerging in the paperfold artefact; proximity, separation, spatial succession, enclosure and contiguity.

The task in this phase is to perceive and configure the space between the folds as actual space. Not yet as the virtual form of a possible building or as an abstract geometric space but as space accommodating an abstract program. A smooth space, that needs to be occupied in order to be calculated.

We introduce the itinerary of a human body, a succession of

movement and stasis as abstract program. Accessibility is the essential operation. Connectivity is consequential performance. Loops and Crossings are emergent space concepts.

Given the consistency of ivory carton, the crease, the pleat and the hinge acquire structural properties in the paperfold artefact. In the folding process of surface warping creases receive and distribute tension and compression. Structural patterns mostly encountered in the development of paper folding techniques are triangulated surfaces of increased variability. The fishbone[6] is a major structural pattern deriving from the domain of origami paper folding, a regular structure susceptible to maximum variability.

Paperfold derivative organizational diagrams are entanglement, interlacement and stratification. Serial variation of strips has been observed as a folding technique that can evolve into an organizational system. Due to the warping of the surface, the dominance of the oblique plane is expressed through a series between horizontal and vertical. Blurred boundaries between spaces indicate constant transformations in conditions of enclosure.

Transition 4: Architectural Prototypes

In a design generative process by folding, the architectural object is not an a priori target to be achieved. Given the educational context, the spatial, structural and organizational diagrams emerging in the process are developed into architectural prototypes. The task here is to attribute architectural properties to the diagram introducing parameters of material, program and context. Thus we can define here as architectural prototype the spatial, structural or organizational diagram that has acquired 'architectural substance'[7].

A concise account of the prototypes developed in the studio course illustrated here includes the warped surface series, the wrapped interior, the niche, intertwining tubes, life-pods for urban nomads, the living-working machine, the hollow dike and the urban camping. Unlike disjunctive notions of cross, trans, or dis-programming[8], attributing architectural substance to the paperfold diagram is a research project that seeks reciprocity between spatial properties, organization of program and structure. Nevertheless this reciprocity goes beyond deterministic interdependence into a multiplicity of possible associations. Through the evaluation of these prototypes we could verify the discursive claim of folding in architecture as a strategy that manages complexity by integration of disparate elements into 'a heterogeneous yet continuous system'[9].

Sophia Vyzoviti, June 2003

Footnotes

1   Ivory carton is direct translation from the Dutch *ivoir karton*; thin, robust but easy to cut white paper available from 90 to 300 g.

2   *Paperfold* is defined here as the result of the process of folding paper, the product of a folding performance.

3   The argument for diagrammatic architecture comes in accordance to Deleuze & Guatarri's notion of the diagrammatic being an intrinsic property of the abstract machine: 'We define the abstract machine as the aspect or moment at which nothing but functions and matters remain. A diagram has neither substance nor form, neither content nor expression.' From **A thousand plateaus - capitalism and schizophrenia**, translation Brian Massumi, University of Minnesota Press, Minneapolis, 1987

4   Stan Allen, 'mapping the unmappable-on notation' in **Practice: architecture, technique and representation**, Critical Voices in art, theory and culture, G+B Arts International, 2000.

5   Gilles Deleuze, **The fold, Leibniz and the Baroque**, trans. Tom Conley, The Athlone Press, London, 1993

6   See also page 18 and 138 of this publication. For further reference consult *Origami Science and Art* - Proceedings of the Second International Meeting of Origami Science and Scientific Origami, Otsu, Japan, 1994

7   Stanford Kwinter, 'The complex and the singular' in **Architectures of Time-Towards a Theory of the Event in Modernist Culture**, The MIT Press, Cambridge Massachusetts, 2001

8   Bernard Tschumi, **Architecture and disjunction**, The MIT Press, Cambridge Massachusetts, 1996

9   Greg Lynn, 'Architectural curvilinearity - the folded, the pliant and the supple' in 'Folding in Architecture', *Architectural Design*, vol.63, Academy Editions, London, 1993

Transition 1
Matter and Functions

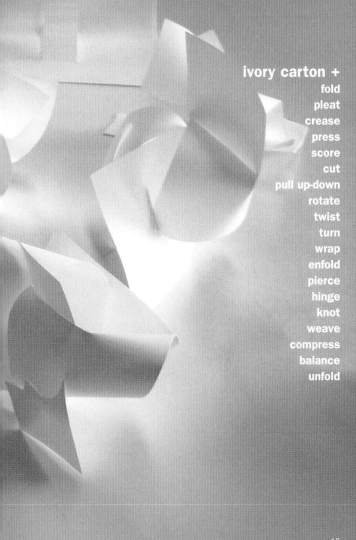

ivory carton +
fold
pleat
crease
press
score
cut
pull up-down
rotate
twist
turn
wrap
enfold
pierce
hinge
knot
weave
compress
balance
unfold

score - crease - fix

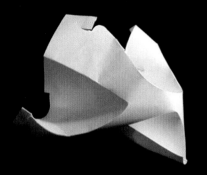

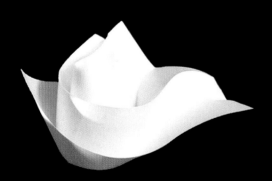

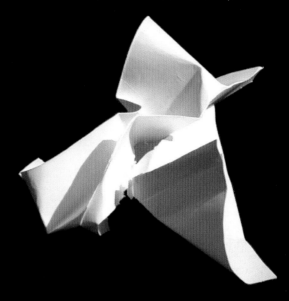

score - cut - unfold - knot

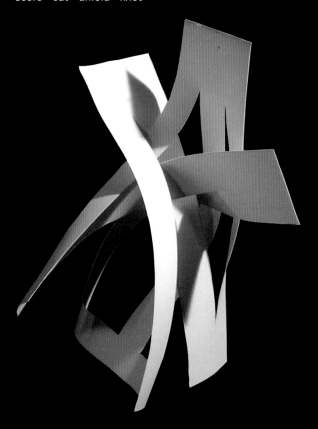

cut - rotate - pierce - hinge

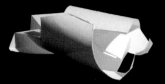

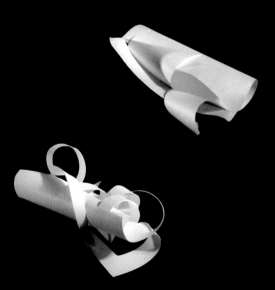

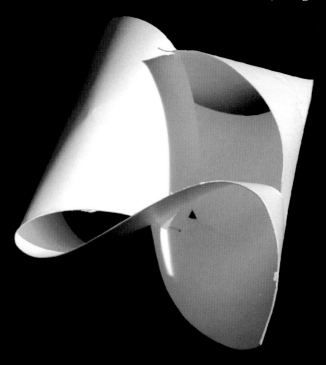

cut - rotate - wrap - hinge

fold - cut - wrap - hinge

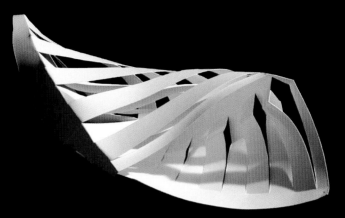

cut - fold - wrap - hinge

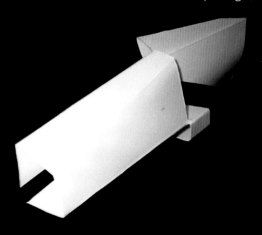

score - cut - fold - hinge

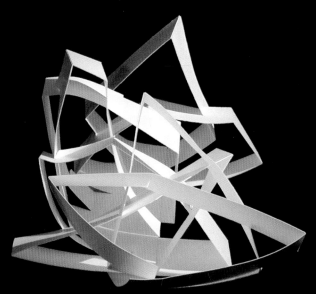

score + cut + fold + hinge

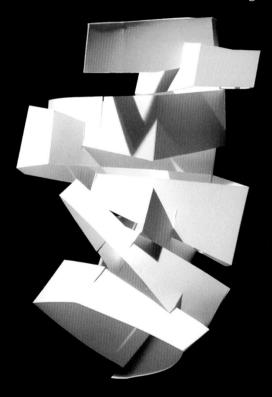

score - cut - cross - hinge

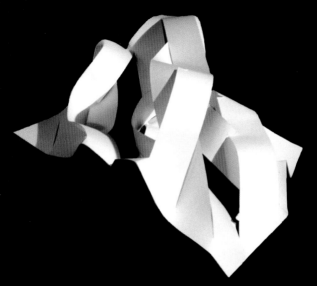

score - cut - fold - rotate - weave

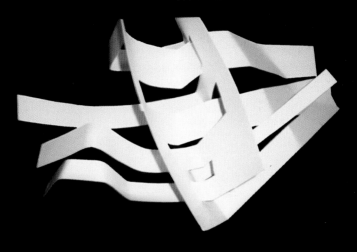

score - cut - fold

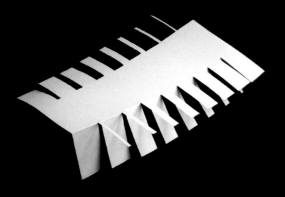

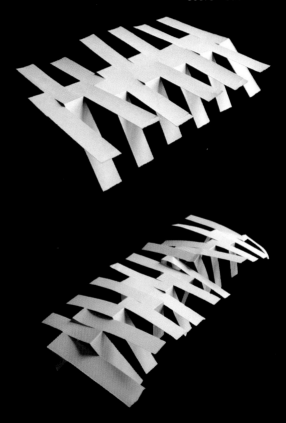

score - cut - fold

score - cut - fold

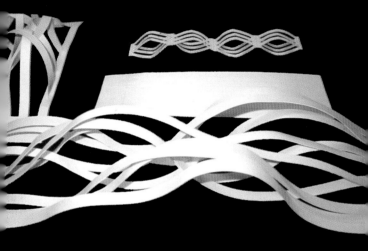

score - cut - pull up

score - cut - unfold

crease - cut - fold - extrude

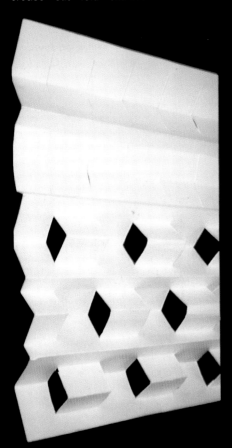

crease - cut - fold - extrude - fold - hinge

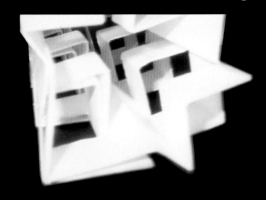

fold - crease - fold - pleat

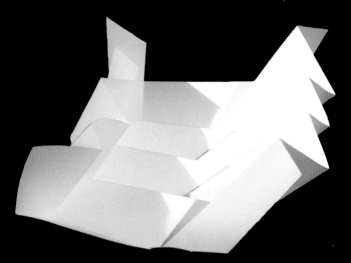

fold - crease - fold - pleat

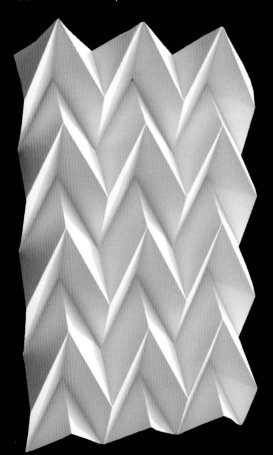

fold - crease - fold - pleat

score - crease - fold

score - crease - fold - compress

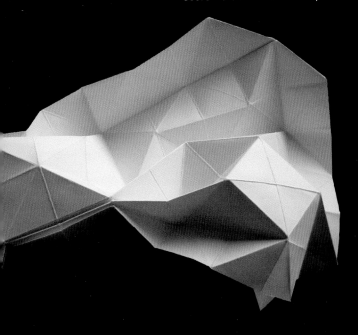

score - crease - fold - unfold

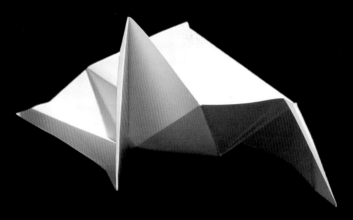

score - crease - fold - wrap

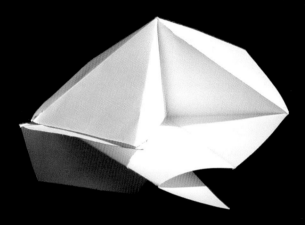

score - cut - fold - crease - cut - balance

score - cut - fold - balance

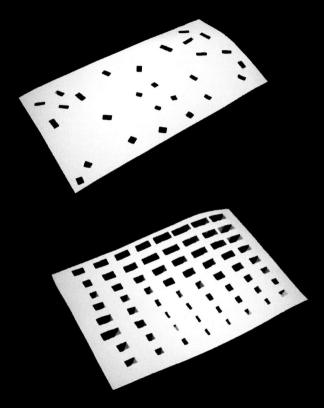

score - cut - fold - balance - crease

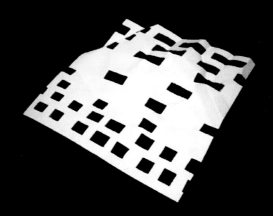

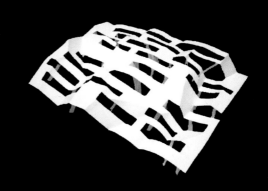

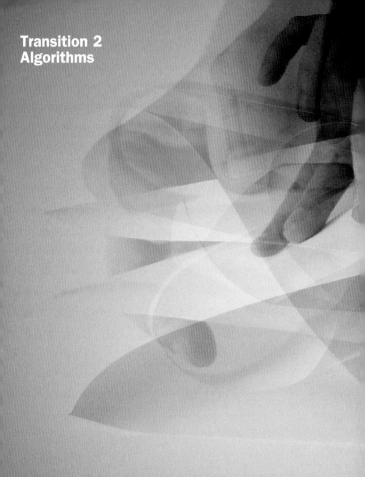

Transition 2
Algorithms

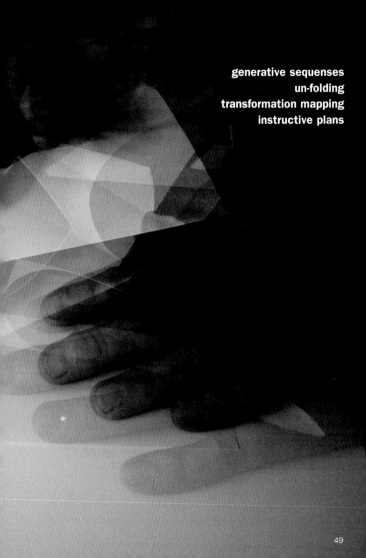

generative sequenses
un-folding
transformation mapping
instructive plans

generative sequence

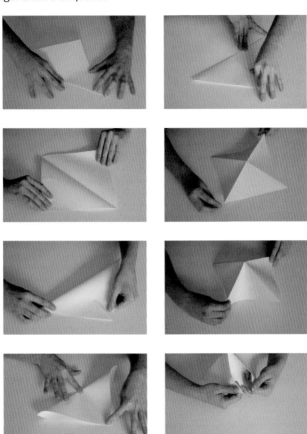

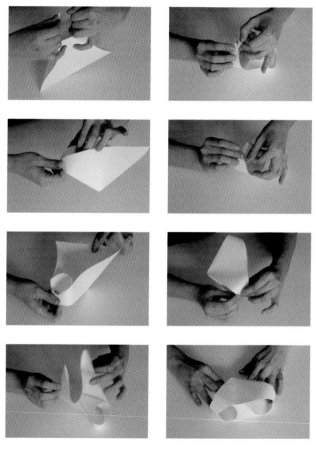

generative sequence

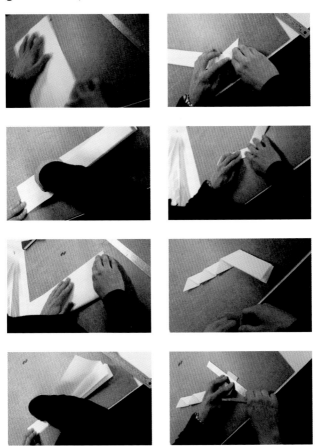

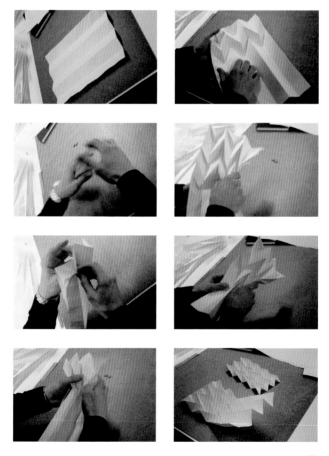

fishbone: direct folding

generative sequence

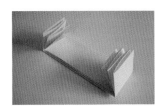

Bas Rozenbeek

unfold: score - cut - fold - pierce

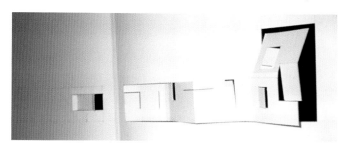

Marcus Buitenweg

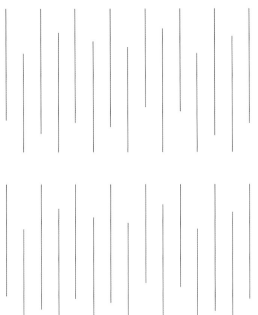

meander: score - unfold

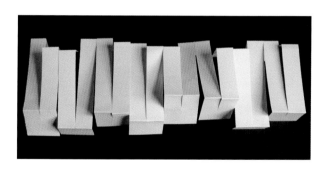

Marcus Buitenweg

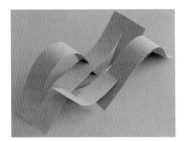

meander: extrusion sequense

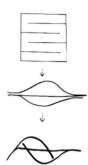

Andreas Lokitek

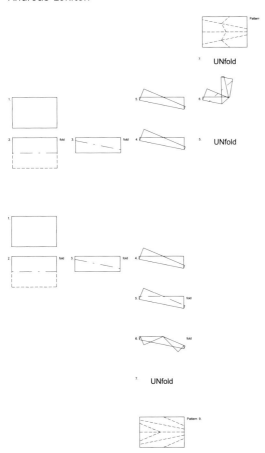

7. UNfold

5. UNfold

5. UNfold

7. UNfold

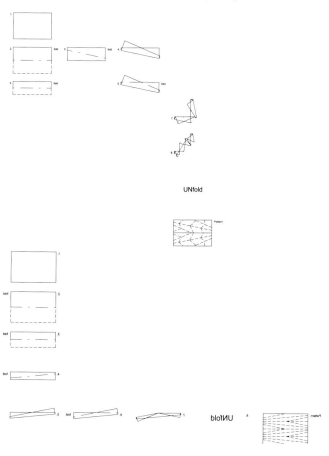

UNfold

UNfold

Ophelie Herranz & Paul Galindo

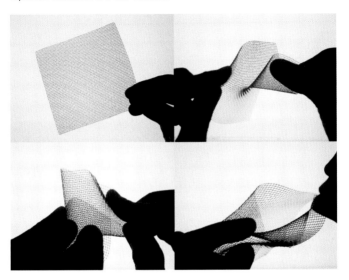

transformation mapping

point d _movement traces

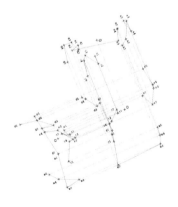

movement traces (all the points)

Bas Vogelpoel

piercing:augmented tecnique - serial variability

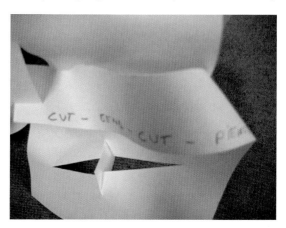

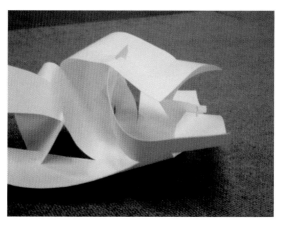

Bas Vogelpoel

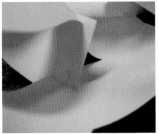

1	-180	-180
	-90	-45
	-90	-45

2	-90	-15
	0	-90
	90	0

3	-180	-10
	-90	-90
	0	-10

4	90	90
	90	40
	0	0

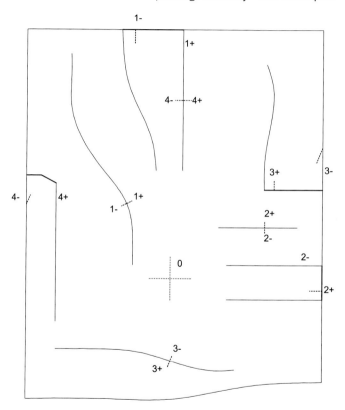

Cindy Wouters

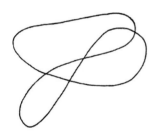

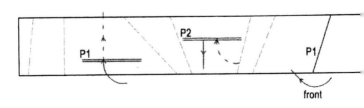

knotted strip: instructive plan

- - - - - -	negative fold
▬▬▬▬▬	incision
————	line where the piercing crosses
P1	piercing 1
- · - · - ·	fold where the piercing crosses

F = front

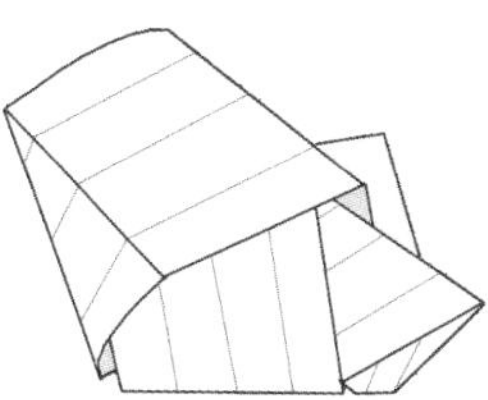

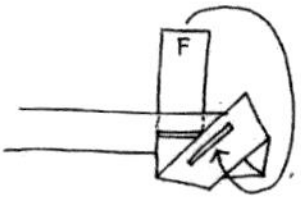

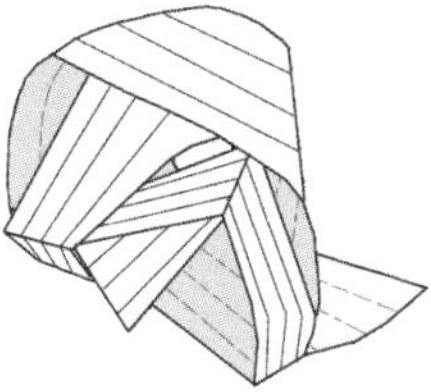

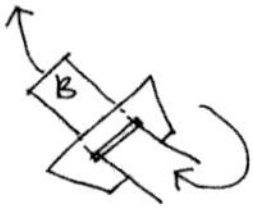

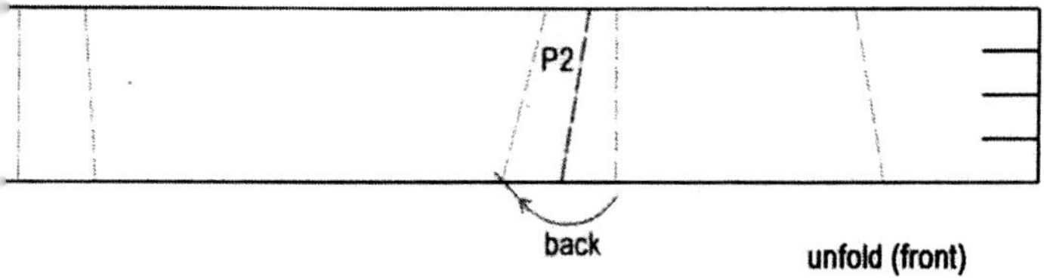

P2

back

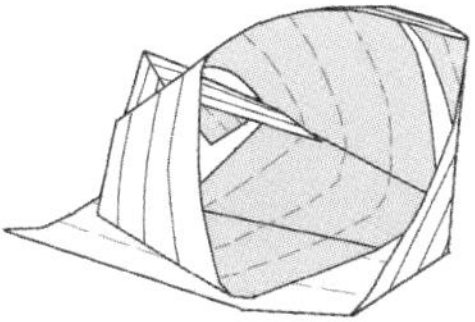

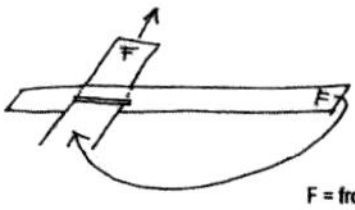

unfold (front)

71

Magnus Bojrkman

oblique section:inventory of transformations

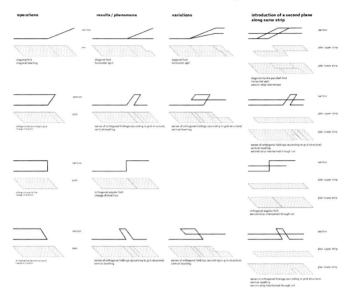

operations	results / phenomena	variations	introduction of a second plane along same strip

section
plan
diagonal fold
diagonal levelling

section
plan
diagonal fold
horizontal split

diagonal fold
horizontal split

section
plan upper strip
plan lower strip
diagonal double parallel fold
horizontal split
second strip intertwined

section
plan
orthogonal parallel joining to grid
change of direction

series of orthogonal foldings (according to grid structure)
vertical levelling

series of orthogonal foldings (according to grid structure)
vertical levelling

section
plan upper strip
plan lower strip
series of orthogonal foldings (according to grid structure)
vertical levelling
second strip intertwined through cut

section
plan
orthogonal angular fold
change of direction

orthogonal angular fold
change of direction

section
plan upper strip
plan lower strip
orthogonal angular fold
second strip intertwined through cut

section
plan
orthogonal parallel joining to grid
change of direction

series of orthogonal foldings (according to grid structure)
vertical levelling

series of orthogonal foldings (according to grid structure)
vertical levelling

section
plan upper strip
plan lower strip
series of orthogonal foldings (according to grid structure)
vertical levelling
second strip intertwined through cut

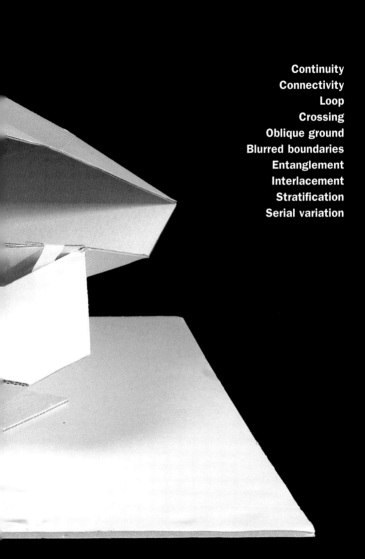

Continuity
Connectivity
Loop
Crossing
Oblique ground
Blurred boundaries
Entanglement
Interlacement
Stratification
Serial variation

Tijs Pulles

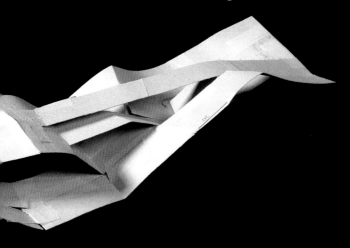

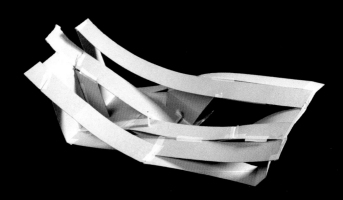

Fredrik Lyth

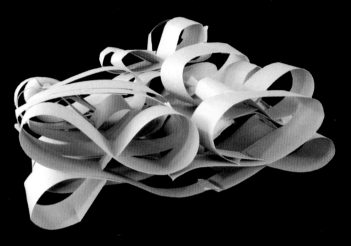

Fredrik Lyth

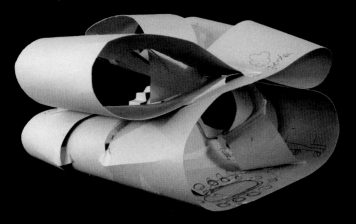

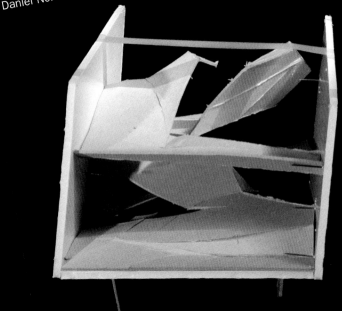
Daniel N...

entanglement - compression

Fokke van Dijk

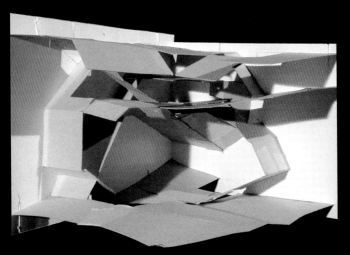

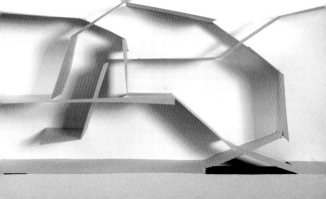

Johan Cederlof

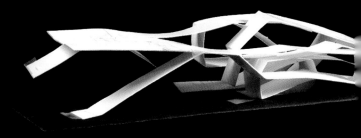

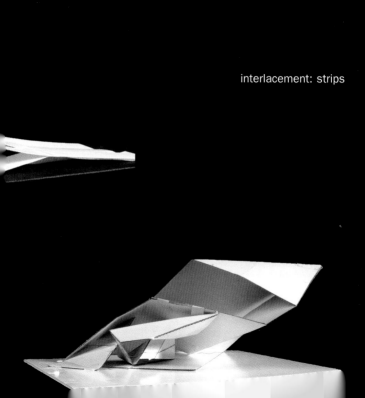

interlacement: strips

Johan Cederlof

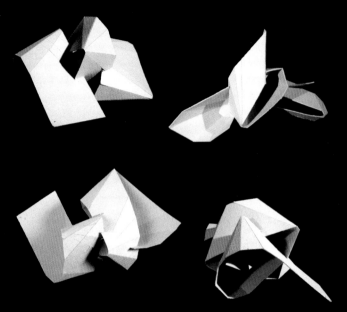

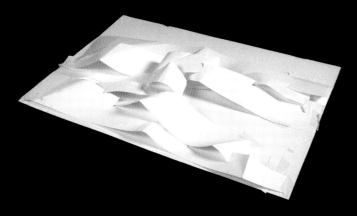

appear... wave + spiral...

something
under (

mother
→ start the wall   in the afternoon - school

end of the highway   northern   enter the
                            light
                                        → direction
underground   dull   lost it

Joost van Boekhold

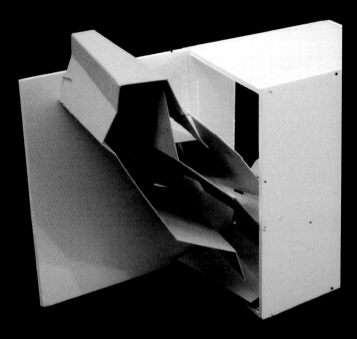

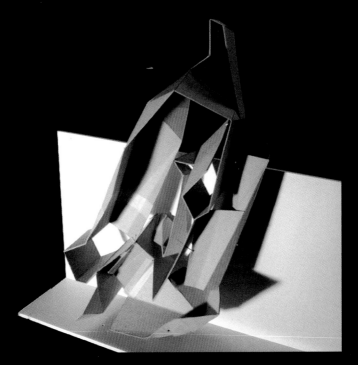

Trine Bang

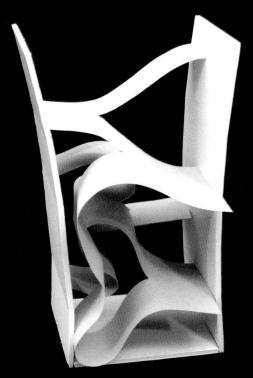

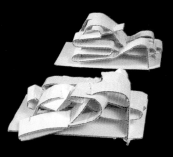
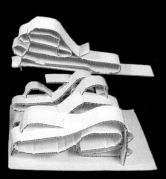

Cristian Veddeler

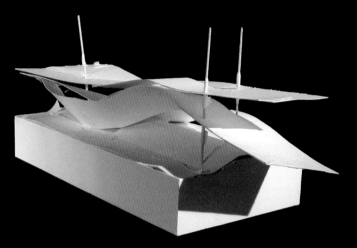

stress forming - enclosure

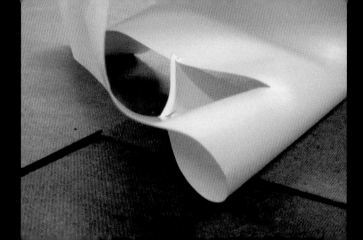

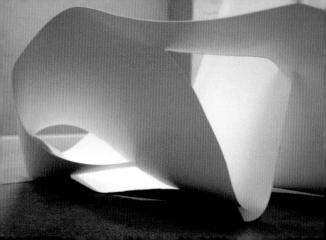

Transition 4
Achitectural Prototypes

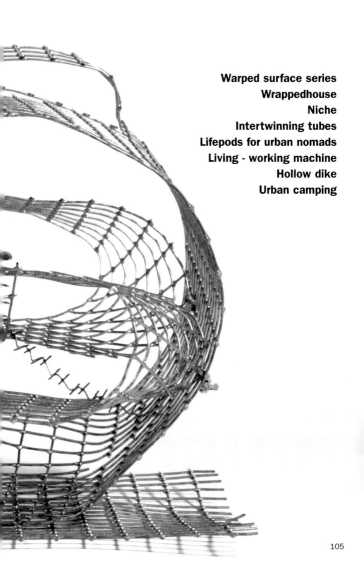

Warped surface series
Wrappedhouse
Niche
Intertwinning tubes
Lifepods for urban nomads
Living - working machine
Hollow dike
Urban camping

Natacha Fricout

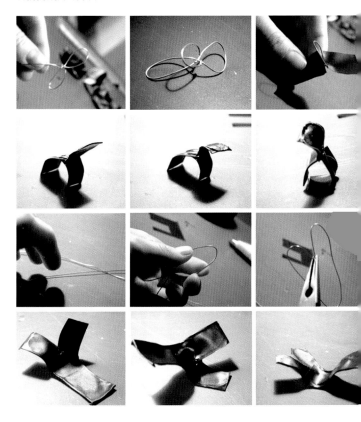

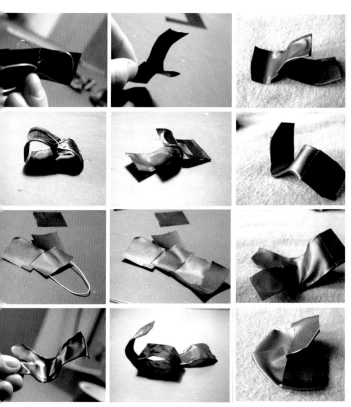

Safia Benayard-Serif

wrapped house: structural prototype

Bas Vogelpoel

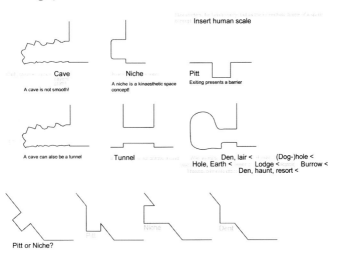

Insert human scale

Cave

A cave is not smooth!

Niche

A niche is a kinaesthetic space concept!

Pitt

Exiting presents a barrier

A cave can also be a tunnel

Tunnel

Den, lair <   (Dog-)hole <
Hole, Earth <   Lodge <   Burrow <
Den, haunt, resort <

Pitt or Niche?

niche: generic plan

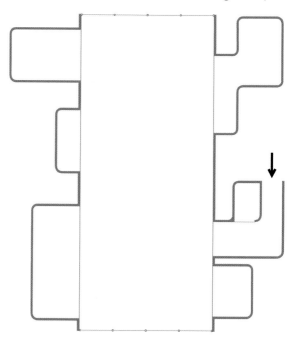

Bas Vogelpoel

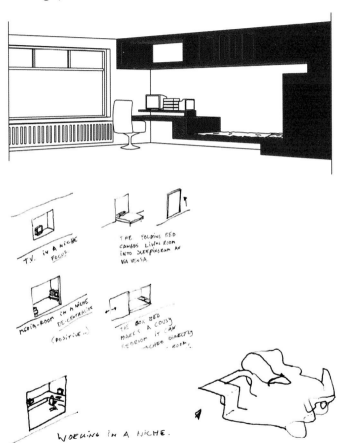

T.V. IN A NICHE
FOCUS.

THE FOLDING BED CHANGES LIVING ROOM INTO SLEEPINGROOM AN VICE VERSA.

MEDIA-ROOM IN A NICHE DE-CENTRALISE (POSITIVE...)

THE BOX BED MAKES A COSY BEDROOM IT CAN ...CHED DIRECTLY ...ROOM.

WORKING IN A NICHE.

i SHOULD CHANGE LIVING AND WORDING FOR SUN ? ??

HOW DO WE UTELIZE THE COMMON. CENTRAL AREA?

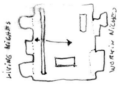

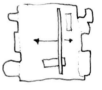

① THE BIG (CLOSET.) WALL THAT SLIDES.

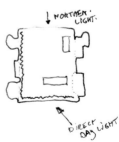

② THE CURTAIN THAT GOES AROUND. AND COMS AROUND.

Johan Cederlof

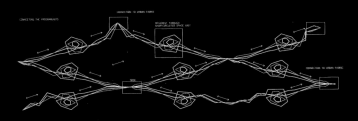

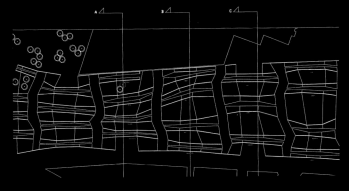

life support

←——→

sociocultural

career

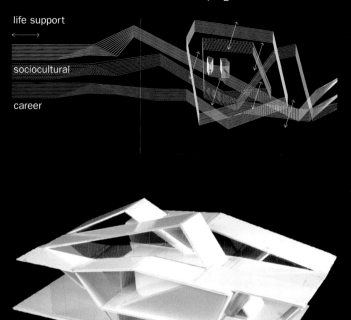

Johan Cederlof

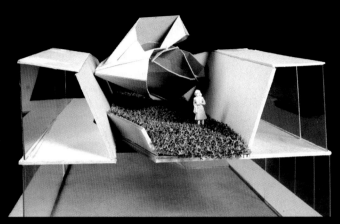

oblique ground: lifepod aggregates

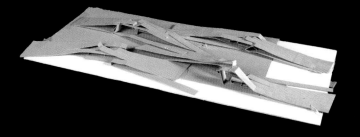

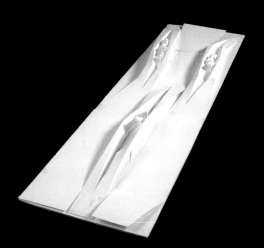

Fredrik Lyth

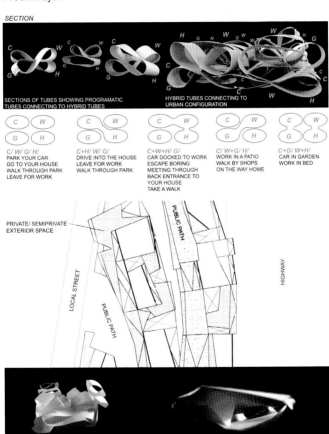

SECTION

SECTIONS OF TUBES SHOWING PROGRAMATIC
TUBES CONNECTING TO HYBRID TUBES

HYBRID TUBES CONNECTING TO
URBAN CONFIGURATION

C/ W/ G/ H/
PARK YOUR CAR
GO TO YOUR HOUSE
WALK THROUGH PARK
LEAVE FOR WORK

C+H/ W/ G/
DRIVE INTO THE HOUSE
LEAVE FOR WORK
WALK THROUGH PARK

C+W+H/ G/
CAR DOCKED TO WORK
ESCAPE BORING
MEETING THROUGH
BACK ENTRANCE TO
YOUR HOUSE
TAKE A WALK

C/ W+G/ H/
WORK IN A PATIO
WALK BY SHOPS
ON THE WAY HOME

C+G/ W+H/
CAR IN GARDEN
WORK IN BED

PRIVATE/ SEMIPRIVATE
EXTERIOR SPACE

PUBLIC PATH

LOCAL STREET

PUBLIC PATH

HIGHWAY

intertwinning tubes

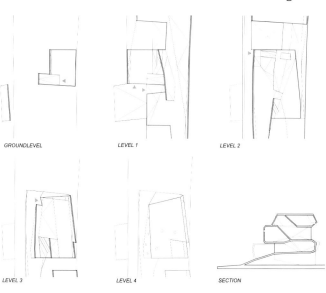

GROUNDLEVEL

LEVEL 1

LEVEL 2

LEVEL 3

LEVEL 4

SECTION

SITUATION

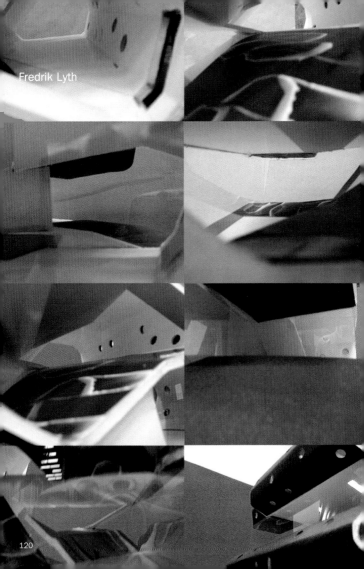

Fredrik Lyth

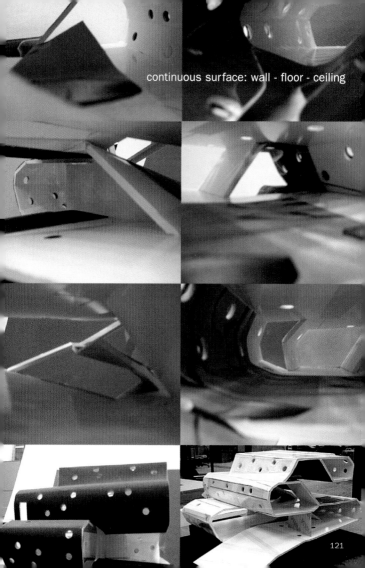

continuous surface: wall - floor - ceiling

Daniel Norell

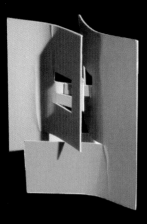

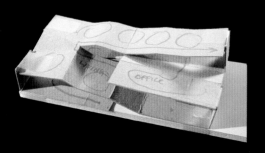

living and working machine: entanglement

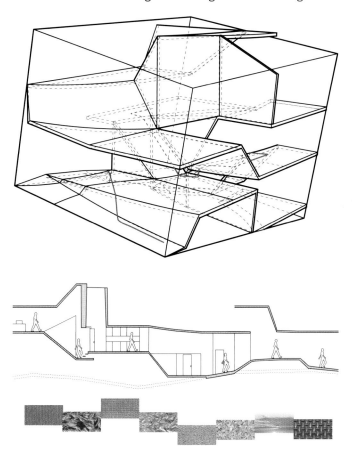

horizontal cuts

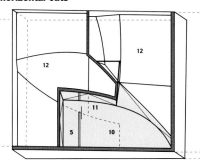

level +8.65 m

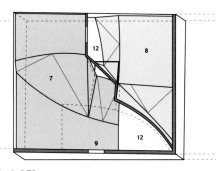

level +6.70 m

living and working machine: developable surfaces

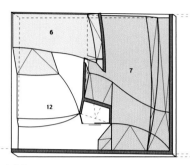

level +4.40 m

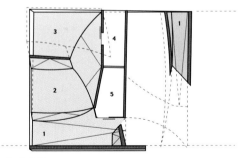

level +2.10 m

1. entrance 2. dining 3. media room 4. storage 5. wc bath/shower 6. cooking
7. working 8. living 9. access upper landscape 10. sleeping 11. roof access 12. void

Cindy Wouters

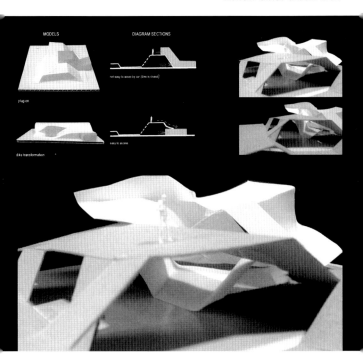

Christian Veddeler

CAMP
SLEEP
EAT
WALK
TALK
CLEAN
SWIM
FUCK
RELAX
SIT
DIVE
CLIMB
SUN
LOOK
BAR- B-Q
COOK
COME
LEAVE
PICNIC

SCALE

PALIMFEST MARKS
URBAN SURROUNDING INFLUENCES
LANDSCAPE SURROUNDING INFLUENCES
MOVEMENT

.SITE

INPUT
PRESSURE

CITY

**WATER
GRASS
ROCK
SUNFLOWERS
TULIPS
APPLETREES
TREES
SAND
STONE
CONCRETE**

Folding Architecture, Concise Genealogy of the Practice

Sophia Vyzoviti

Folding emerged as an architectural discourse aspiring to become the new architecture of the end of the 20th century. In the perspective of a concise genealogy we can consider the Architectural Design Profile, guest-edited by Greg Lynn, *Folding in Architecture*[1] its early manifesto. The issue released in 1993 comprises an anthology of essays and projects by a group of architects seeking an alternative to the contradictory formal logic of Deconstructivism, and includes among others

Cobb, Eisenman, Gehry, Kipnis, Lynn and Shirdel. Featuring an excerpt from Deleuze's, at that time recent English translation, *The fold, Leibniz and the Baroque*[2]; *Folding in Architecture*, draws philosophical substance from the work of Deleuze, a radical understanding of Leibniz, employing the Baroque as a theoretical tool to analyze contemporary artistic and intellectual movements.

Greg Lynn, in his contribution to the above issue, titled - 'Architectural curvilinearity - the folded, the pliant and the supple', introduces folding as a third architectural response to complex and disparate cultural and formal contexts, operating neither by conflict and contradiction as Deconstruction nor by unity and reconstruction as Neo-Classicm, New-Modernism and Regionalism. Etymologically relating complexity with pliancy [3], the architecture of the fold is considered a cunning tactic for intensive integration of difference within a heterogeneous yet continuous system, working beyond addition by smooth layering, a concept demonstrated with analogues from geology as mineral sedimentation, and culinary mixing techniques. Forms of viscosity and pliability are considered its new instruments: forms that are sticky and flexible, 'where things tend to adhere to'. For Lynn curvilinearilty is the formal language of 'pliant architecture'. Husserl's unexact geometries are essential for the comprehension of pliant forms: rigorous geometries that in contrast to exact geometries, cannot be reproduced identically, are irreducible to average points or dimensions but can be determined with precision.

As a paradigm for geometry of multiple probable relations Lynn introduces the supple topological surface of Rene Thom's catastrophe graph.

In *The fold, Leibniz and the Baroque* [4] Deleuze submits a set of Baroque traits that stretching outside its historical limits are contributing to the appreciation of contemporary art. Considering them crucial for the understanding of the evolution of the discourse on the fold into a practice of folding architecture these traits are summarized:

1. The fold: the infinite work in process, not how to conclude but how to continue, to bring to infinity.
2. The inside and the outside: the infinite fold separates or moves between matter and soul, the façade and the closed room, the inside and the outside.
3. The high and the low: being divided into folds, the fold greatly expands on both sides thus connecting the high and the low.
4. The unfold: not as the contrary to the fold but as the continuation of this act.
5. Textures: as resistance of the material, the way a material is folded constitutes its texture.
6. The paradigm: the fold of the fabric must not conceal its formal expression.

Deleuze regards inflection as the ideal generic element of the variable curve of the fold. Quoting his student Bernard Cache, he defines the point of inflection as an 'intrinsic singularity' involving three transformations: vectorial, projective and infinite variation. In this frame Cache argues for a new definition of the technological object, the 'objectile' as an event-assuming place in a continuum by variation where industrial automation or serial machineries replace stamped forms. This new status of the object no longer refers to a spatial mould but to a temporal modulation that implies as much the beginnings of a continuous variation of matter as a continuous development of form. In *Earth moves: the furnishing of territories*[5], published in 1995 Bernard Cache proposes to re-define architecture as a folded practice of interior and exterior relations and as the art of the frame. Cache sets the conditions for the new in architecture by the 'inflection image' focusing on furniture as hinge between geography and architecture.

Perhaps the most influential unexecuted project of the 90's and probably the earliest to transcribe Deleuzian traits in an architectural design are *2 Bibliotheques at Jussieu*, Paris by OMA in 1993. In this competition entry for the public library on the university campus folding is employed both as organizational diagram and a spatial device that produces density. Koolhaas uses the metaphor of the 'the social magic carpet' addressing the continuous floor surface of the building. The floors slabs are sloped to coincide with the superceding and underlying ones, producing a continuous path, 'a warped interior boulevard that exposes and relates all programmatic elements' thus transforming the library experience into that of an urban landscape. Folding as a spatial device abolishes the 2.5-meter human occupation heightconstraint while instigating a *flaneurie* through the library interior. In *S,M,L,XL*[6] the paperfold is not only illustrated as a concept model but also introduced into the practice as a new architectural strategy and imagery.
The design exemplifies architecture neglecting the idea of the façade, rather concentrating on the floor as a catalyst of spatial connectivity and social interaction.

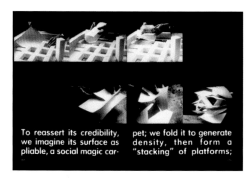

To reassert its credibility, we imagine its surface as pliable, a social magic carpet; we fold it to generate density, then form a "stacking" of platforms;

Investigating the origins of *Jussieu's* continuous sloped floors we should acknowledge as precedents Virilio's concepts of the oblique ground and habitable circulation. Paul Virilio and Claude Parent published in 1966 *Architecture Principe*, a series of architectural and urban manifestos. Here Virilio develops the

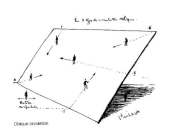

Oblique circulation

theory of the 'oblique function', an angular plane that constitutes the 'third spatial possibility for architecture' subverting the norms of horizontal and vertical oriented space. The *oblique plane* is considered the instigator of a tactile relationship between building and body primarily activated by disequilibrium. The *oblique* is idealized as the field where the corrupted by the static architecture of horizontal-vertical intense spatial perception is re-gained, by a kind of eroticization of the ground. 'Architecture will no longer be dominated by the visual, the façade, but will relate to the human body as a receptive totality'. The oblique plane alters the relationship of space and weight: gravity affects perception since 'the individual will always be in a state of resistance- whether accelerating as going down or slowing down as climbing up, whereas when one walks on a horizontal plane weight is nil'[7]. Virilio claims the origins of the theory of the oblique in his childhood explorations. Interiors of upturned or tilted bunkers on the coast of Normandy provided his first experiences of 'unstable spaces'. The oblique plane, as third axis in the Euclidean system, offers the opportunity for habitable surface and circulation to become one continuous space. The allocation of human activities on sequences of oblique surfaces, cannot be exactly defined but require a geometry of multiple probable relations, including zones of predictability of activities as in Thom's catastrophe curves that are constrained by percentage of inclination and material texture.

The oblique plane as habitable circulation will prove to be one of the most fertile concepts in the evolution of innovative Architecture in the nineties, admittedly a prolific decade in respect to folding. The *Jussieu* library project fertilizes the folding discourse into architectural practice, spawning a series of single surface projects in a generation of architects worldwide. Particularly in the Netherlands the oblique floor acquires tectonic substance in a number of projects becoming a simulation of a landscape. Since an exhaustive enumeration of such designs would exceed the limits of a concise survey only a few references will proceed. The continuous slopped surface evolves within OMA's practice into the folded floor.

Kunsthall, Rotterdam 1993, comprises a knot of paths, circulation spaces involving different kinds of movement: exhibition visitors, passers by and vehicles. The folded concrete floor manifests tectonic mastery in the *Educatorium*, Utrecht 1997, a central facility shared by the faculties of the

University of Utrecht. Described by Bart Lootsma 'the *Educatorium* brings about an entirely new kind of spatial experience in which is hard to tell where the exterior ends and the interior begins. Passing through doors without noticing the transition, one does not observe any staircases or even thresholds- visitors glide into the building. Once inside, movement is imperceptible from one level to another, even though staircases are here and there, where vertical distance to be bridged is sufficient to warrant one.'[8]

If we consider flow as a prerequisite of a continuous surface, the garage as well as the Guggenheim Museum of Modern Art would qualify as architectural prototypes of inhabitable circulation. Vehicular movement as an overriding architectural program is the ideal brief for a folded organization. Avoiding repeated reference to the car, another paradigm of the oblique continuous plane as a superseding architectural element would be bicycle parking. The *bicycle-flat* or *fietsflat* in Dutch designed by Amsterdam based VMX Architects in 1998 and completed construction in 2001, is conceived as a continuous-enfolded

bicycle path. In the process of infrastructure upgrading, the Amsterdam municipality decided to free the entrance plaza of its Central Railway Station from the mass of bicycles, by installing temporary storage for 2500 bicycles. VMX architects proposed a three level self-supporting, de-mountable structure consisting of a continuous strip unfolding in length to 110 meters. Bicycles can be stalled on both sides of the track. The architects state that the design is based on a very functional storage: 'Using the existing height difference along the station square of 1,25 meters a system of slopes (3 degrees) has been created on which the bicycles can be stored. Red asphalt will be laid over the slopes like a carpet. Short cuts for going up do exist in a number of bicycle stairs, but undoubtedly cyclists will prefer to go down using the ramp. The expression of the building will be made by an efficient detailing and material choice, but chiefly by the sculptural form of the slopes.'[9] Despite this, the building in its performance appears to be transgressing the infrastructural efficiency of the bicycle-storage to become a new kind of public space and a contemporary icon for the city of Amsterdam. Besides the mass of commuters, the *bicycle-flat* hosts a number of other visitors: tourists, filmmakers and bmx-freestylers, whose presence supports Virilio's claim for inhabitable circulation as an instigator of social interaction.

Having elaborated on the continuous oblique surface, a major feature of folding architecture, a new notion will be exemplified further through the folded texture: the fabric revealing its form. A reference to the work of Diller + Scoffidio serves as an ideal introduction here.

In *Bad Press* folding materializes as a process resulting in the re-configuration of the masculine shirt as a critique to standardization and a subversion of the constitution of contemporary self-image. In the winning competition entry for *Eyebeam*, Museum of Art and Technology in New York [10] completed in 2002 the folded strip is deployed both as spatial and organizational diagram.

The new *Eyebeam* building will house a museum of art and technology, artist-in-residence studios, education center, multi-media classrooms, state-of-the-art Theater and digital archive. The facility will provide unprecedented production and exhibition opportunities for artists exploring new media in video, film and moving image art, DVD production, installation, 2D/3D digital imaging, net art and sound and performance art forms. The double folded strip displays the buildings formal

determination; it provides the interface for the digital media space and encloses its supporting infrastructures. The pleated section of the *Eyebeam* building computes. It is a plexus of technological infrastructures and their interfaces, into an intelligent architectural smoothly layered skin.

The final reference in this survey embraces an emergent architectural paradigm of a folded organization, considering the projects scale and influence: the Port Terminal at Yokohama Osanbashi Pier, completed in 2002 by Foreign Office Architects.

In their 1995 winning international competition entry, *Yokohama Port Terminal*, architects Alejandro Zaera-Polo and Farshid Moussavi delivered a single surface prototype where folding traits permeated all scales of the design. The urban proposal introduced the continuous ground as a mechanism for the penetration of urban space on the terminal's roof and an instigator of a public space at the interface of terminal functions and city events. It has been described by the architects as '…a public space that wraps around the terminal, neglecting its symbolic presence as a gate, de-codifying the rituals of travel and a functional structure which becomes the mould of an a-typological public space, a landscape with no instructions of occupation' [11].

The cruise terminal program, consisting of a bundle of diffuse and directed movement including the flows of citizens, passengers, visitors, vehicles and luggage, is organized by the layering and interlacing of paths. The building's formal determination manifests a topological surface concept in sequences of inclined curvilinear spaces that accomplish smooth transitions between programmatic elements. The structural and construction principles intensify the overriding spatial concept by assigning the origami folded steel plate as the structural principle thus demolishing the traditional separation between building envelope and structure.

During the seven years implementation period of the project the stress has shifted towards research based construction pragmatics. As Alejandro Zaera-Polo states 'the structural development of the project has become the main source of ideas for its implementation and a trail of discovery that reaches far beyond the images that have become the better known side of the project'[12]. Research on engineering processes in different levels was conducted in collaboration with Japan based SGD engineers. A series of alternative structural prototypes where developed before resolving to the combination of girders and a folded plate structure. An origami archetype, the fishbone pattern is the origin of the folded plate

visible on the roof of the terminal's halls. Origami structure can be appreciated as regional reference supporting 'the introduction of context as a process of material organization rather than image'. Even though the fishbone comprises a regular generic structure, every unit in the specific folded plate is differentiated. Following the terminal's geometric guidelines that are themselves inflected; the geometry of the pattern is tangential to the circles regulating the complex curvilinear girders, constantly varying in a lesser degree. Thus the structural pattern extends through an infinite series of variability.

In conclusion, *Folding Architecture - Concise Genealogy of the Practice* has registered the effect of the discourse of the fold in the practice of architecture focusing on a small number of landmark projects that have essentially contributed to its evolution in the 10 years following 1993. The purpose of this survey was to ground the studio research *Folding as a Morphogenetic Process in Architectural Design* in a theoretic and professional framework.

This genealogy has, however, omitted a line of work intersecting Deleuzian discursive traits with computer generated design, narrowing the perspective to end of 20th century techniques. Given the opportunity of an extensive survey an update on the recent work of Bernard Cache and Greg Lynn would be fundamental.

The traits introduced by Deleuze stimulated the thinking of a generation of architects. Consequently the fold has acquired architectural substance, manifested tectonic properties and can be delivered now as design knowledge. The attributes of the new architectural object emergent in the re-definition of the practice are contended below in a set of propositions:

1. Extension: the object as an infinite series, serial variability
2. Multiplicity: the object as a plexus of elements, potential interactivity
3. Curviliniarity: inflection, obliqueness, warping of surfaces and non Euclidean geometries
4. Stratification: layering and interfacing between contradicting architectural factors
5. Continuity: topological properties of surfaces and organizational principles
6. Fluidity: interlacement of boundaries, fuzzy demarcations and zones of probability

By which I can submit *the fold, Deleuze and the re-definition of the practice*, as an alternative title which may further the research presented in this essay F*olding Architecture - Concise Genealogy of the Practice*. Given the fact that a new generation of architects is being educated on the foundation of this discourse we can only expect an even more rigorous and innovative performance in the future.

Footnotes

1   'Folding in Architecture', *Architectural Design*, vol.63, Academy Editions, London, 1993

2   Gilles Deleuze, **The fold, Leibniz and the Baroque**, trans. Tom Conley, The Athlone Press, London, 1993. Originally published in French as **Le Pli: Leibniz et le baroque**, 1988

3   ibid. 'Folding in Architecture', Greg Lynn, 'Architectural curvilinearity - the folded, the pliant and the supple'
    'The unforeseen connections possible between differentiated sites and alien programs require conciliatory, complicit, pliant, flexible and often cunning tactics. Presently numerous architects are involved with the heterogeneities, discontinuities and differences inherent within any cultural and physical context by aligning formal flexibility with economic, programmatic and structural pliancy. A multiple of pli based words- folded, pliant, supple, flexible, plaited, pleated, placating, complicitous, compliant, complaisant, complicated, complex and multiplicitous to name a few- can be evoked to describe this emerging urban sensibility of intensive connections.' (p.11)

4   Ibid. Gilles Deleuze, **The fold, Leibniz and the Baroque**

5   Bernard Cache, **Earth moves: the furnishing of territories**, trans. Anne Boyman, ed. Michael Speaks, Massachusetts Institute of Technology, 1995

6   Rem Koolhaas & Bruce Mau, **S,M,L,XL**, 010 publishers, Rotterdam, 1995

7   Enrique Limon, an interview with Paul Virilio, 'Paul Virilio and the Oblique', in **Sites and Stations - Provisional Utopias**, S. Allen and K.Park eds., Lusitania Press, New York, 1995

8   Bart Lootsma, **SUPERDUTCH**, Thames and Hudson, London, 2000

9   'Fresh facts', Netherlands Architecture Institute, Rotterdam, 2002

10 www.eyebeam.org/museum/arch.html

11 Foreign Office Architects - 'Yokohama International Port Terminal', *AA Files* no.29, London, 1995

12 Alejandro Zaera-Polo, 'Roller coaster construction', *verb_architecture boogazine*, Actar, Barcelona, 2001

Colophon

Author
Sophia Vyzoviti
Concept
Joost Berkhout and Sophia Vyzoviti
Graphic design
Mariëlle Tolenaar / studiosap
Printer
Star Standard Industries Ltd, Singapore

About the author
Sophia Vyzoviti, born in Thessaloniki in 1971, is an architect practicing in Greece and the Netherlands. She is Design Instructor and Lecturer at the Faculty of Architecture- Delft University of Technology, Tilburg Academy for Architecture and Urbanism and the School of Architecture- University of Thessaly. Her work has been exhibited in the National Pavilion of Greece, Venice Biennale 2000 and more recently smoothcity was part of the 'Mobility Laboratory' of International Architecture Biennale Rotterdam 2003. Sophia Vyzoviti received the Diploma of Architect-Engineer at the Faculty of Architecture- Aristotelian University of Thessaloniki in 1994 and a Master in Architecture at the Berlage Institute in 1997. Since 1999 she has been research associate at Design Knowledge Systems, Faculty of Architecture - Delft University of Technology.